D1716352

JESUS
AND THE
Miracle
OF THE
MASS

Gracie Jagla

Illustrated by Randy Friemel

Huntington, Indiana

Nihil Obstat
Msgr. Michael Heintz, Ph.D.
Censor Librorum

Imprimatur
✠ Kevin C. Rhoades
Bishop of Fort Wayne-South Bend
July 27, 2022

The *Nihil Obstat* and *Imprimatur* are official declarations that a book is free from doctrinal or moral error. It is not implied that those who have granted the *Nihil Obstat* and *Imprimatur* agree with the contents, opinions, or statements expressed.

Every reasonable effort has been made to determine copyright holders of excerpted materials and to secure permissions as needed. If any copyrighted materials have been inadvertently used in this work without proper credit being given in one form or another, please notify Our Sunday Visitor in writing so that future printings of this work may be corrected accordingly.

Copyright © 2023 by Gracie Jagla

28 27 26 25 24 23   1 2 3 4 5 6 7 8 9

All rights reserved. With the exception of short excerpts for critical reviews, no part of this work may be reproduced or transmitted in any form or by any means whatsoever without permission from the publisher. For more information, visit: www.osv.com/permissions.

Our Sunday Visitor Publishing Division
Our Sunday Visitor, Inc.
200 Noll Plaza
Huntington, IN 46750
www.osv.com
1-800-348-2440

ISBN: 978-1-68192-017-9 (Inventory No. T2755)
1. JUVENILE NONFICTION—Religious—Christian—Inspirational.
2. JUVENILE NONFICTION—Religious—Christian—Devotional & Prayer.
3. RELIGION—Christianity—Catholic.

LCCN: 2022940154

Cover design: Lindsey Riesen
Cover and inteior art: Randy Friemel
Interior design: Tyler Ottinger

PRINTED IN THE UNITED STATES OF AMERICA

To my grandparents and my Sophia Thérèse

GRACIE JAGLA

To all children preparing for first Communion

RANDY FRIEMEL

Look up to the altar,
And what do you see?
What seems like plain bread
In the priest's hands is me!

My child, I am Jesus,
And I love you so.
I have a great story
I'd like you to know.

You've heard about miracles,
So big and so grand —
Great signs and wonders
That come from God's hand.

It might seem they all
Happen so far away.
But what if I said
You could see one today?

A miracle happens
At each Catholic Mass
That shakes the whole church,
From pews to stained glass.

Here in the Eucharist,
I come visit you!
And I bring all of Heaven
Right down with me, too.

You might not feel different
Or sense that it's me.
It looks like bread and wine,
But I'm hidden here — truly!

For if you went to Mass,
And you saw with my eyes,
You'd see all of Heaven
Right there in disguise!

So, come on with me —
I'll lend you my view.
It takes eyes of faith
To believe that it's true.

As the Mass begins,
You're preparing your heart.
I'm watching with joy
From the moment you start.

The priest proceeds in,
And he places with care
A kiss on the altar,
For I'll soon be there.

And during the readings,
My words are alive.
I am speaking to you
Before I arrive.

As the altar is set,
I think of that night
Before I gave you
The gift of my life.

I took bread and wine
And held them both up,
Saying, "This is my body
And blood in this cup."

"You must do this again
In remembrance of me,
So there's no time or place
Where I will not be."

From that moment on,
Through apostles to priests,
I've been present with you
At this holy feast.

When the priest says the words,
That small bread becomes me!
My body, blood, soul,
And my divinity.

The God who created you,
Who came down to earth,
Who's known all your thoughts
From your moment of birth …

Is coming to you!
Just close your eyes.
Fling open your heart,
One, two, three — and surprise!

Flash! Comes a starburst
Of sparkling light
From out of the host.
It's my heart shining bright.

Down from the rafters
Fly angels of mine,
Swirling above
And then falling in line.

The saints and
past loved ones

Come squeeze in
your pew.

Tell them hello,

They're here praying
with you!

And this moment's so great,
You are burst out of time
Into Heaven's realm
When the altar bells chime.

As time fades away,
You are brought into one
With the Church past and future.
Here Heaven has begun!

Events from my life,
From my passion to glory,
Are here re-presented.
You're part of my story.

Now's the best part —
When you come receive me!
It's the reason for all
I have done; do you see?

I wrap you up strongly
And hold you so tight.
You're joined with my heart
And start glowing with light.

Your soul starts to glitter,
And shine with gold rays.
You become like a monstrance:
A place where I stay.

In this holy moment,
Your chance is right now
To talk to me freely.
Give your head a bow.

Imagine your best friend
Is sitting by you.
What would you say to him?
What would you do?

Tell me your stories,
The good times you've had.
Times you've been happy
And times you've been sad.

Then sit here in silence
And listen awhile
To the ways I love you
And how you make me smile.

The most precious gift
In my whole world is you!
I'd die once again
Just to show you it's true.

Each Mass keeps my promise
To always stay close
And be there for you
When you need me the most.

Now, go out to the world
And remember you're mine.
When people see you,
They'll see my light shine!

OSV Kids

Helping families love and live the Catholic Faith

OSV Kids is an exciting new brand on a mission to help children learn about, live, and love the Catholic Faith. Every OSV Kids product is prayerfully developed to introduce children of all ages to Jesus and his Church. Using beautiful artwork, engaging storytelling, and fun activities, OSV Kids products help families form and develop their Catholic identity and learn to live the faith with great joy.

OSV Kids is a monthly magazine that delivers a fun, trustworthy, and faith-filled set of stories, images, and activities designed to help Catholic families with children ages 2-6 build up their domestic churches and live the liturgical year at home.

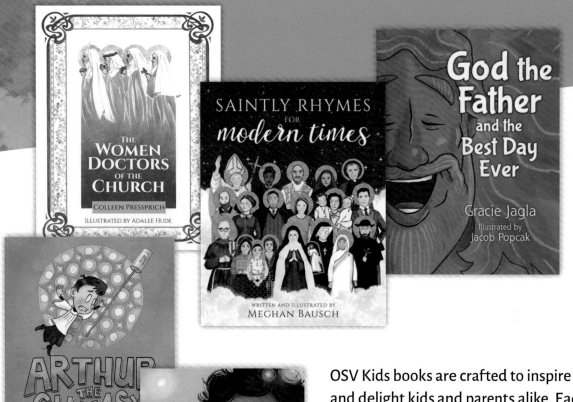

OSV Kids books are crafted to inspire and delight kids and parents alike. Each book is designed to kindle the Catholic imagination within young readers through creative storytelling, stunning artwork, and fidelity to the Church's teachings. With board books for infants and toddlers, picture books for young readers, and exciting stories for older kids, OSV Kids has something for everyone in your family.

Learn more at OSVKids.com

About the Author

Gracie Jagla is a wife and mother of two little girls. Besides staying home with her children, writing is one of her greatest joys! She writes faithful Catholic books infused with a dash of imagination and a sprinkle of grace. Her prayer is that her books bring families closer to Christ and make God smile in the process. She is also author of *God the Father and the Best Day Ever* (OSV, 2020) and *The Night the Saints Saved Christmas* (OSV, 2021).

About the Illustrator

Artist Randy Friemel resides in Texas, where he is known for creating liturgical and Christian art since 2009. Friemel is best known for his Christian art, and feels it is the highest calling of all artists. Having made illustrations for several kids' books, Friemel prefers using oils to create scenes and make things happen, and he enjoys the texture in the end result.